Who Was Isaac Newton?

Who Was
Isaac Newton?

by Janet B. Pascal

illustrated by Tim Foley

Penguin Workshop

For Professor Owen Gingerich, whose demonstration of
Newton's third law I will never forget—JPB

PENGUIN WORKSHOP
An imprint of Penguin Random House LLC, New York

First published in the United States of America by Penguin Workshop,
an imprint of Penguin Random House LLC, New York, 2014

Text copyright © 2014 by Janet B. Pascal
Illustrations copyright © 2014 by Tim Foley
Cover illustration copyright © 2014 by Penguin Random House LLC

Visit us online at penguinrandomhouse.com.

Library of Congress Control Number: 2014952920

Printed in the United States of America

ISBN 9780448479132   20 19 18 17 16 15

Contents

Who Was
Isaac Newton?

In 1665, a terrible sickness swept through
England. It was called the plague. It caused huge
swellings all over the body and made people's skin
turn black. There was no cure. Most people who
caught it died a quick and painful death. Any
place people lived crowded together was dangerous,

because plague was very easy to catch. No one knew what caused it, or how to protect themselves against it. The only way to stay safe was to go to the countryside, where there were fewer people to catch it from.

A twenty-three-year-old student named Isaac Newton had to leave Cambridge University and flee to his mother's farmhouse. He didn't really mind. He had always been a loner. He didn't have friends he would miss. At his mother's house, he spent the time doing what he did best—thinking about the universe.

One day he saw an apple fall. He began to wonder what pulled the apple toward the Earth. And so, according to the famous legend (which might even be true), young Isaac Newton thought up the idea of gravity.

The plague years were a terrible time for most people, but not for Newton. For him, they were a wonderful time of discovery, and not just about gravity. He came up with enough new ideas to keep him busy thinking and writing for the rest of his life. His ideas helped people understand how the universe worked in a new way.

After eighteen months, Newton went back to Cambridge, but he never did make many friends. He was jealous and unfriendly, and he lost his temper easily. He wasn't a very nice person, but he was one of the greatest scientific geniuses who has ever lived.

ISAAC NEWTON

Chapter 1
Lonely Boy

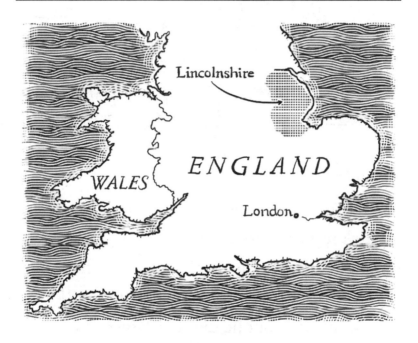

Isaac Newton was born in Lincolnshire, England, on Christmas Day 1642. (Because England used a different calendar then, his birthday is also given as January 4, 1643.)

He didn't seem to have a great future. At first,
it didn't seem he had any future at all. He was
born too early. He was weak and so tiny he could
fit into a quart mug. No one thought the sickly
baby would live, but he did. His father, also
named Isaac, had died three months before his
son's birth. He had been a well-off farmer, but he
couldn't read or write—not even enough to sign
his name.

THE ENGLISH CIVIL WAR

NEWTON WAS BORN RIGHT AT THE BEGINNING OF THE ENGLISH CIVIL WAR. DURING HIS CHILDHOOD, THE KING AND PARLIAMENT WERE LOCKED IN A BLOODY STRUGGLE. IN 1649, WHEN NEWTON WAS SIX, KING CHARLES I WAS PUT ON TRIAL AND BEHEADED. A STRICT GOVERNMENT WITH NO KING TOOK POWER. ELEVEN YEARS LATER, IN 1660, THE MONARCHY WAS RESTORED UNDER CHARLES II. ALTHOUGH NEWTON'S FAMILY WAS NOT PERSONALLY INVOLVED IN THE WAR, THE VIOLENCE AND UNCERTAINTY OF THE TIME HAD AN IMPACT ON HIS CHILDHOOD.

When Isaac was only three, his mother, Hannah, got married again, to a minister named Barnabas Smith. Smith wanted a wife, but not a son. Hannah agreed to move into her new husband's house, leaving Isaac behind with her parents.

Little Isaac almost never saw his mother, and he was very lonely. Sometimes he would climb a tree so he could stare at his mother's new home. He hated his stepfather so much that he imagined burning down the house with him in it. When Isaac was ten, however, his stepfather died.

His mother moved back, bringing with her a half
brother and two half sisters for Isaac.

Isaac went to the little local village school, which didn't teach much beyond how to read. He seemed unusually intelligent, so Hannah decided to send him to a better school. The King's School

was seven miles away—too far to walk—so Isaac lived with the Clarke family in town. The family later said that while he lived there, Isaac fell in love with Clarke's daughter Catherine. If this is true, she was the only girlfriend he ever had.

Years later Catherine remembered him as "a sober, silent, thinking lad" who was never known to "play with the boys . . . at their silly amusements." In his spare time, he built doll furniture for Catherine.

Clarke was an apothecary. An apothecary is someone who makes medicine by combining herbs and chemicals. This involved careful work with weights and measures, as well as knowing what was special about different substances. Young Isaac was fascinated. By watching and perhaps helping Clarke, he began to learn basic

chemistry—how different things interact with each other. He even created his own potions, such as a medicine made up of turpentine, rosewater, beeswax, olive oil, a kind of wine called sack, and red sandalwood. This was meant to protect him from a deadly disease called tuberculosis.

Isaac was also fascinated by ways to keep track of time. The clocks of the day weren't very accurate, and he thought he could do a better job. He charted the movement of shadows from sunrise to sunset. Then he hammered pegs into the wall to create a sundial. When people wanted

to know the real time, they'd check "Isaac's dial."
For telling time indoors, he designed a clock with
a wooden dial turned by the steady dripping of
water. He also built a tiny windmill, with a mouse
to run it.

Unfortunately, the subjects taught at school didn't interest him. He didn't study, and he was at the bottom of his class. One day a boy who was a good student kicked him in the stomach. Isaac immediately challenged him to a fight, which, to everyone's surprise, he won. Isaac was very good at holding a grudge. Just winning the fight wasn't enough for him. He wanted to beat his enemy in school as well, so he finally began to study. Soon he rose to the top of the class.

The main subjects at school were Latin and Greek. Both would be useful to him later on, because almost all the most important books and articles were still written in these languages. He may have also learned some simple, useful arithmetic and geometry.

Hannah thought of education mainly as a way to make her son a good farmer. Soon she decided it was time for him to practice running a farm, so she took him out of school. The idea of growing crops and taking care of animals bored Isaac. He deliberately did a bad job.

When he was supposed to be working, he sat under a hedge reading or building things. Once when he was supposed to watch the sheep, he let them run into a neighbor's field and eat the crops.

His mother was hauled into court and had
to pay a fine after that happened. Isaac was not
turning into the kind of farmer his mother
hoped for.

Chapter 2
Cambridge

Luckily, Isaac wasn't the only one who hated the idea of his becoming a farmer. The master of his school thought it was a waste of a brilliant mind. Along with Isaac's uncle, he managed to talk Hannah into letting her son go to a university. So at eighteen, Isaac Newton left for Trinity College. This was part of Cambridge University. He would spend the next forty years living there, first as a student and then as a professor.

Newton's first months at Cambridge were a letdown. Even though Hannah was well-off, she didn't want to pay his fees, so he had to enter as what was called a sizar. This meant he worked as a servant to the richer students.

Most of them were more interested in having a good time than in learning. Newton despised them. He grew less lonely when he met another serious student, John Wickins. They moved in with each other and lived together for the next twenty years.

Wickins was one of the few people Newton ever stayed friends with for long. Unfortunately Wickins never wrote down his memories of Newton.

Study at Cambridge was still based on ancient Greek and Latin philosophy, especially the writings of the Greek philosopher Aristotle. Aristotle was a brilliant man—the Newton of his time—but he had lived in the fourth century BC. Over two thousand years later, knowledge in many areas hadn't moved much beyond what he taught.

Aristotle based his theories on observation of the world around him. However, it was even more important to him for an idea to make sense. He didn't always test his ideas against reality. For instance, he thought that human males, being bigger and stronger, would have more teeth than human females. That seemed

ARISTOTLE

CAMBRIDGE

IN NEWTON'S TIME, VERY FEW PEOPLE ACTUALLY GOT TO GO TO COLLEGE. THERE WERE ONLY TWO UNIVERSITIES IN ALL OF ENGLAND: OXFORD AND CAMBRIDGE. BOTH WERE ANCIENT. THEIR MAIN PURPOSE WAS TO PREPARE STUDENTS TO BE MINISTERS IN THE CHURCH OF ENGLAND, AND ONLY MEMBERS OF THE CHURCH WERE ALLOWED TO ATTEND THEM. EVERY STUDENT HAD A PERSONAL TUTOR WHO TOOK CHARGE OF HIS EDUCATION. MANY OF THE UPPER-CLASS STUDENTS, HOWEVER, WERE ONLY THERE TO HAVE A GOOD TIME.

reasonable to him. If he had actually looked in men's and women's mouths, he would have seen that he was wrong. In the centuries after his death, other scholars often just accepted what Aristotle had said as the truth.

Much of what was taught at Cambridge didn't interest Newton, and he paid little attention to it. What Cambridge did offer was a library full of books.

Over the past few centuries, daring scholars had been challenging the old ways of explaining how the world worked. The word *scientist* hadn't been invented yet—these scholars were known as natural philosophers. They became the founders of modern science. Newton set out to learn from them.

Newton read the ideas of Nicolaus Copernicus, one scholar who challenged Aristotle. Aristotle thought that the Earth was the center of the universe and all the other heavenly bodies moved around it. In the sixteenth century, Copernicus suggested it made more sense to think that the Earth and all the other planets moved around the sun. This seemed reasonable to Newton.

NICOLAUS COPERNICUS

Aristotle's idea felt right—it certainly looks to us like everything revolves around the Earth. But anyone who actually watched the planets in the sky could see that sometimes the way they moved didn't match what Aristotle described.

People came up with all sorts of complicated ideas to explain why the planets didn't behave as Aristotle said they should. But if they stopped trying to force the planets into Aristotle's system and switched to Copernicus's system,

ARISTOTLE'S THEORY

COPERNICUS'S THEORY

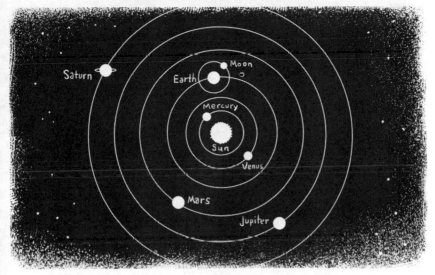

with all the planets traveling
around the sun, everything
suddenly made sense.
The planets moved just
the way Copernicus's
theory predicted.

Newton also read
the work of Johannes
Kepler, who had built
on Copernicus's work.

JOHANNES KEPLER

Copernicus had suggested that planets moved in circles around the sun. Kepler tracked the planets' movements carefully and discovered

their exact paths. They were not circles but a kind
of oval called an ellipse.

GALILEO

Then there was Galileo, an Italian who died the year Newton was born. He looked at the heavens through a telescope and reported on the surprising things he saw. For instance, the moon was covered with mountains and craters, and there were spots on the sun. Aristotle said that heavenly bodies must be pure and more perfect than anything on Earth. What Galileo actually saw made him disagree. Even out beyond the moon, it looked as if things were made of the same ordinary material as on Earth.

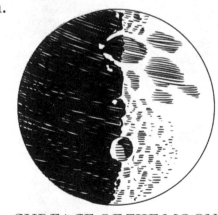

SURFACE OF THE MOON

Galileo believed in testing the truth of what other people told him. For instance, Aristotle said that heavy objects fell faster than light objects. That certainly sounds reasonable, but Galileo wondered if they really did. He came up with experiments to find out, by dropping balls and measuring how fast they fell. According to legend, Galileo dropped balls from the leaning Tower of Pisa. That isn't so. Nevertheless, he did discover that Aristotle was wrong. Objects of the same size and shape, dropped from the same height, fall at the same speed, no matter how much—or how little—they weigh.

From reading these men's works, Newton learned something. It didn't matter how reasonable an idea seemed. It had to match what could actually be observed. If the world didn't do what an idea said it would, it was time to come up with a new idea.

At Cambridge, Newton began to teach himself mathematics. This interest grew out of a visit to Stourbridge Fair. The fair was a huge outdoor gathering with farmers and tradesmen selling everything from farm animals to clothing to toys. Full of young couples, dancers, and performing animals, it was a much more frivolous place than Newton usually liked. But he did find a bookseller there, and he bought a book on astrology.

Astrology is the belief that the stars and planets rule people's lives. Astrologers use the heavens to predict the future and try to control events on Earth. Astrology had become very complicated, using elaborate calculations and charts.

Many people in Newton's time believed in astrology, so he was curious about it. Before he had read very far in his new book, Newton came to an example that used a kind of difficult mathematics he didn't know. He bought another book to teach himself about it. But before he could understand this new book, he had to know a more basic branch of mathematics that he hadn't learned yet. So he had to back up and start at the beginning.

In 1665, Newton passed the exams for his bachelor's degree. His grades were not very good. Most of the exam questions were about subjects that didn't interest him. Still he did well enough to become a scholar. This meant he could keep living and studying at Cambridge, with free room and board. Almost as soon as he earned the right to stay at Cambridge, however, he had to leave.

Chapter 3
The Plague Years

In 1665, the plague broke out in England. The university was closed, and Newton went home to Lincolnshire.

For the next eighteen months, he lived at home. Newton had never much liked being with other people. He was happy to be left alone to think about exactly what he wanted. This was the most productive time of Newton's life. He later remembered, "In those days I was in my prime of age for invention." By *invention* he meant being able to think up new ideas.

What was he thinking up? A new kind of mathematics, to start with. The math he knew was fine to use for some kinds of problems. If you knew how fast a wagon was going and that it was moving in a circle, it was easy to figure out where it would be an hour later. However, Newton was interested in a different kind of problem. He wondered about things that were changing all the time. What if you shot a cannonball into the air? First it would travel in a curve upward, slowing down more and more. Then it would get to the top of its path and start curving back down toward the Earth. As it got nearer to the ground, it would move faster and faster. Its speed and its direction were always changing. How could you create a mathematical equation that would describe this kind of movement when it was never the same for an instant?

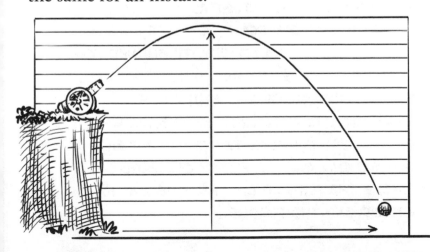

THE PLAGUE AND THE GREAT FIRE

WHEN THE PLAGUE STRUCK, LONDON BECAME
A CITY OF DEATH. AS MANY AS ONE IN FIVE
PEOPLE WERE KILLED BY THE DISEASE. THEN
IN SEPTEMBER 1666, JUST AS THE PLAGUE WAS
BEGINNING TO DIE DOWN, A GREAT FIRE BROKE
OUT. STARTING IN A BAKERY, IT BURNED FOR
THREE DAYS. MOST PEOPLE MANAGED TO ESCAPE,
BUT 80 PERCENT OF THE BUILDINGS IN LONDON
WERE RUINED. ALTHOUGH NO ONE KNEW IT, THE
PLAGUE WAS CARRIED BY RATS AND FLEAS. BY
DESTROYING ALL THE FILTHY OLD BUILDINGS
WHERE THE RATS LIVED, THE FIRE MAY HAVE
HELPED END THE PLAGUE.

Newton invented his own form of mathematics—one that could handle this kind of question. He called it the *method of fluxions*. Fluxion means "continual change." Today we call his invention calculus. Modern physics, the study of motion, matter, and energy, would not be possible without it.

Another subject that always interested Newton was light. He had bought himself a prism at Stourbridge Fair. This was a specially shaped piece of glass. When light shone through it, the light turned into a rainbow of color. (We call this the spectrum.) Newton began playing around with his prism, testing what he had learned about light.

Aristotle taught that in its basic form, light was pure white. All other colors came from making changes to white light. If you changed it a little, you got red. Changing it a little more gave you orange, and so on through all the colors. But by now, Newton knew Aristotle was sometimes wrong. Maybe he was wrong about light.

Newton knew that when you shine white light through a prism, the light breaks up into all the colors of the spectrum. What would happen if you sent the broken-up spectrum through a second prism? If white light was really being changed to turn into all the colors, a second prism should change the light even more. Newton discovered that, in fact, this didn't happen. A second prism brought all the colors back together to create a single beam of white light again.

This made Newton think of other questions. What would happen if you shone just a single color of light through a second prism? He created an experiment to find out. First he passed a ray of white light through a prism, to get the whole spectrum. Then he took just the green light and sent it through a second prism. If Aristotle was right, the first prism had already done something to the white light that had turned it green. What would the second prism do? Would it break the green light up into the whole spectrum again? Would it just change the green a little more, so it turned blue? Instead, Newton discovered that the second prism made no change at all. The green beam stayed green.

His experiments told Newton that Aristotle was wrong. White light was not the basic form of light. Instead, white light was made up of all the different colors put together. The prism wasn't making changes to the white light. It was breaking it up and separating it into its different parts.

From what he figured out about light, Newton was able to explain a mystery. Until Newton, no one understood what made rainbows appear in the sky. Newton realized that drops of water in the air could act like prisms, breaking the white light of the sun into red, orange, yellow, green, blue, indigo, and violet. He was able to explain how, when sunlight passed through these natural prisms, it created a rainbow.

Chapter 4
Falling Apples

Newton's year at his mother's house came to be called his *annus mirabilis.* In Latin that means *miraculous year.* It seemed like a miracle that one young man could figure out so much in so short a time. Discovering the true nature of light and inventing calculus was just the beginning. He also began the work that would lead to the laws of motion named after him and to the theory of gravity. The famous story about Newton tells how a falling apple led him to discover gravity. This story may even be true. In his later years, Newton himself said his first notion of gravity was "occasioned by the fall of an apple," and there were apple trees at Woolsthorpe.

Aristotle taught that the reason things fall is

because heavy objects have a natural tendency to move downward. Again it seemed to Newton that Aristotle was wrong. He didn't think it made sense to say that objects had a built-in need to fall down. He thought there must be some kind of force that pulled things toward the Earth.

If there was such a force, how far up could it reach? Newton decided that maybe the force didn't have any limits. The very same force that pulled on the apple could also be pulling on the moon and the planets as well.

This was a brand-new and amazing idea. In Newton's time, people thought the universe was divided into two parts. There were forces that worked here on Earth and there were forces out beyond the moon. They were completely different. Because people couldn't travel to outer space, there was no way to study these forces. This meant no one could ever learn how the universe worked beyond the small part people could reach.

Now Newton had decided that if he studied the falling apple, he could learn about the forces at work on everything in the universe. The more he thought about it, the more certain he became. The force that made an apple fall from a tree was the very same force that made the moon circle around the Earth instead of flying off into space.

No one knows exactly how far Newton got in figuring out all these ideas during his miraculous year, or how much he worked out later. It was a long time before Newton shared his thoughts with anyone else.

All his life Newton hated going public with his discoveries. He didn't like to tell anyone else until he was positive he had worked out every detail perfectly. He wanted to be sure no one could possibly catch him making a mistake. He also seemed to like keeping his bold, exciting ideas all to himself.

Chapter 5
The Wonderful Telescope

When the plague finally ended in 1667, Newton went back to Cambridge. Here one of his teachers encouraged him to share at least one of his discoveries with the world. This teacher was Isaac Barrow, the first-ever professor of mathematics at Cambridge.

ISAAC BARROW

In 1669, Newton showed Barrow a paper he had written on his method of fluxions. Barrow was amazed by this wonderful new mathematical tool. He thought it was too important for Newton to keep all to himself.

Newton reluctantly let Barrow show the paper to a very small number of people, but he absolutely refused to let it be published.

In October 1669, Barrow left Cambridge. He thought so highly of Newton that he arranged for Newton to take his place as professor of mathematics. Thanks to Barrow, Newton was finally able to live exactly the kind of life he wanted. His duties didn't take much time or energy. All he had to do was give a few lectures. He was a very dull lecturer and difficult to understand. Almost no one went to hear him.

Newton didn't care. He wasn't interested in the other students or professors. He spent most of his time wandering around the university in badly fitting clothing, with his long silver hair hanging uncombed.

Newton was often so busy thinking that he would forget whether or not he had eaten. The rumor at Cambridge was that his cat got fat from the meals Newton left sitting on his table. He slept only a few hours a night and often not in his bed.

Newton wanted to learn more about the way planets moved. To do this, he needed a powerful telescope, but the telescopes of his time weren't good enough for him. They worked by collecting light from a wide area and then focusing it through a glass lens. The images they produced were fuzzy, with a fringe of colors.

Newton wanted a telescope that gave a clearer image. He used what he had discovered about light to solve the problem. The trouble was the lens, he realized. When white light passed through a lens, the lens acted like a prism and broke the light into separate colors. This caused the light to become unfocused, and the image would blur.

Newton had read about another possible way to make a telescope, one that used a mirror. This might get around the problem, because the light would be reflected, instead of passing through a lens. But no one had ever managed to actually build such a telescope.

Newton had loved to build models when he was a child. He used the skills he had learned then to make a reflecting telescope that worked as well as telescopes ten times its size.

Chapter 6
Fighting about Light

Newton's wonderful telescope caught the interest of an important club in London. It was called the Royal Society. Founded in 1660, this was a group of scholars who met every week to watch experiments and talk about science.

The Royal Society thought the best way to advance knowledge was to discuss ideas, so each man could build on—

NVLLIVS IN VERBA

or knock down—what the others were thinking. Their motto was *Nullius in verba*, which means roughly, "Don't take anyone's word for it."

Clubs like the Royal Society were springing up all over in Newton's time. This period is often called the Age of Enlightenment. *Enlightenment* means learning the kind of important knowledge that changes the way people think. The great scholars of the time believed in working together. They wanted to deal with issues of all kinds using reason, logic, and observation—not superstition or religion.

Newton is considered one of the Enlightenment's greatest figures, but his personality didn't fit the Enlightenment ideal very well. He didn't want advice from other people. He wanted to keep his work to himself until it was perfect. Even then, he hated talking about it with other people. If they questioned him—or even worse, thought he might be wrong—he lost his temper.

Still it was flattering for Newton to have such an important group interested in his telescope. He let himself be persuaded to share. In 1671, Barrow displayed the telescope in London, where it was a huge hit—even with the king. Newton donated a telescope to the Royal Society. In return, the society made him a member.

Joining the Royal Society in 1672 led Newton to take another important step. He would try to behave more like an Enlightenment scholar. Instead of keeping his research secret, he would share it with others. He sent the fellows of the Royal Society a paper about the research on light he had done five years earlier. He couldn't resist bragging a little about how important the work was. He proudly described it as "the oddest if not the most considerable detection which hath hitherto been made in the operations of nature." He described the experiments he had done and asked the society members to see if they could get the same results.

At first, all seemed well. One member wrote to Newton that his paper had "met with a singular attention and uncommon applause." However, not everyone agreed with everything he said. They had questions. Some people tried his experiments and claimed they didn't work. Newton felt as if

ROBERT HOOKE

they were attacking him, and he fought back.

One member of the Royal Society in particular made him very angry. This was a man named Robert Hooke. His job was to demonstrate experiments at the society's meetings. Hooke actually agreed with much of what Newton said. But he didn't believe that Newton's experiments really proved what Newton said they did.

Disagreement of this kind is common among scientists—it's an important way to work out the problems with an idea and to make new discoveries. Unfortunately, both Hooke and Newton were very sensitive and proud. They didn't just discuss ideas—they had fights. As the arguments grew worse, they insulted each other, and each accused the other of stealing ideas. They became enemies for life.

Newton never learned to enjoy give-and-take arguments with his fellow scholars. He missed working alone, entirely for his own satisfaction. "I desire to decline being involved in such troublesome & insignificant Disputes," he proclaimed. He went back to working all by himself.

Chapter 7
A Secret Life

Arguing with other scholars was not Newton's only problem. He also had a more personal difficulty. Newton was a fellow of Cambridge University. Being a fellow meant the university gave him money to live and work there, safe from the world outside. Cambridge was part of the Church of England. Every fellow had to become a minister in the church within seven years. By 1674, Newton's seven years were almost up. But he couldn't become a minister because, secretly, he didn't accept the teachings of the church.

Newton was a Christian and very serious about his religion. However, being Newton, he wasn't willing to just accept someone else's explanation about anything important.

Newton read the Bible with the same fierce, questioning mind he turned on the natural world. He decided that he did not agree with the Church of England about the Holy Trinity. The church said that God was one being, made up of the Father, the Son, and the Holy Ghost, and all three were divine. To stay at Cambridge, Newton would have to swear that he accepted this idea. But he didn't—he thought it was wrong to call Christ God. If he refused to agree with what the church said, he would be forced to leave Cambridge in disgrace, but he didn't want to lie about something so important.

In 1675, he approached King Charles II. He thought the king might be able to help him because he was the head of the Church of England. Newton didn't want to tell the king the real reason for his problem. Instead he explained that he wasn't just a fellow of the university. He was also a professor of mathematics.

KING CHARLES II

According to Newton, this meant he should not have to become a minister. This argument didn't really make sense. Fortunately, King Charles didn't care. Newton didn't have to become a minister, the king decided. He was able to stay at Cambridge without having to lie.

Just as he had a secret religious life, Newton also had a secret scientific life. He wanted to unlock the mysteries of alchemy. Alchemy was part magic, part religion, and part science. In secret, alchemists searched for the Philosopher's Stone, which would turn other metals into gold, and the Elixir of Life, which would grant immortality.

Newton spent even more time and energy on alchemy than he did on ordinary science. His servant reported that Newton often sat up all night in his private lab at Cambridge, bent over a roaring fire, working on mysterious experiments.

This might seem odd and puzzling. Why was a scientist involved with secret rituals and magic? Actually, it's not hard to guess why alchemy might appeal to him. He hated to have his work criticized in public. Alchemy offered him a perfect excuse to keep it secret. Alchemists considered themselves special, much wiser than ordinary people. Newton liked seeing himself as part of this select group.

But there was more to Newton's interest than that. In Newton's time, science was still in an early stage. It was not always possible to separate myths from facts. Alchemists believed they could turn other metals into gold because they thought that everything was made up of tiny particles that could be separated and recombined to make something else.

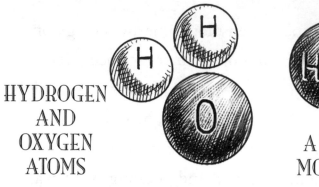

HYDROGEN AND OXYGEN ATOMS

A WATER MOLECULE

The questions the alchemists asked were not foolish. Some of their knowledge would eventually lead to modern chemistry and contribute to our knowledge of how atoms combine to form molecules.

Still, this was the Age of Enlightenment. Serious thinkers were turning away from the idea of special, secret wisdom available only to the chosen few. After Newton died, the Royal Society discovered he had written over a million words about alchemy. They were so embarrassed by this that they marked the papers "not fit to be printed." Newton's writings about alchemy were not published until 2004.

Chapter 8
A Competition

After his fight with the Royal Society, Newton withdrew into himself. He concentrated on his secret study of alchemy. He claimed he wasn't interested in scientific research anymore. Maybe he meant what he said at the time, but his greatest work was still ahead of him.

In 1684, three members of the Royal Society were chatting in a coffeehouse about current scientific issues. These three were Newton's enemy Hooke, a young astronomer named Edmond Halley, and Christopher Wren,

EDMOND HALLEY

a famous architect. Wren had been trying to understand how and why planets orbited the sun. Now he asked the other two men for help.

CHRISTOPHER WREN

People already knew what path an orbiting planet actually followed. Johannes Kepler had shown in 1609 that it was an ellipse. They also knew that the amount of force between the planet and the sun decided the path of the orbit. But something else was involved that no one could figure out. The strength of the force changed in a complicated way, depending on how far apart the two bodies were. The force got weaker as the planet and the sun got farther apart. That made sense, but the force and the distance didn't seem to change at the same rate.

The force changed faster and faster the more the distance grew. No one could figure out exactly what the relationship between the distance and the force was.

Scholars had come up with various ideas to explain the relationship. One suggestion was a mathematical relationship called the inverse square rule. Wren thought this might be the right one, but he had tried to prove it, and he couldn't.

Wren put the problem to his friends. Could they prove—using mathematics—that the inverse square rule would produce an elliptical orbit? If so, they would have created an important new law about the way the planets moved.

Hooke bragged that he had already done this, but he wasn't ready to tell the others how. First he wanted them to try and fail. Then he would show them. Wren and Halley didn't take Hooke very seriously. (When Newton had produced his wonderful telescope, Hooke claimed that *he* had already made a telescope that worked even better and was so small he could hang it from his watch chain.) Wren offered a prize—a valuable book—to whoever could show him the mathematical proof first.

After two months, Hooke still hadn't shown him anything. Nervously, Halley decided to approach the prickly Newton. Like Hooke, Newton said he had already proved that the inverse square rule would produce an elliptical orbit, years before. Unfortunately he wasn't sure where he had put the proof. He had only done it for his own amusement. He promised to send it to Halley as soon as he found it. Unlike Hooke, Newton wasn't just bragging. Within a few months, Newton was able to send Halley his proof.

HALLEY'S COMET

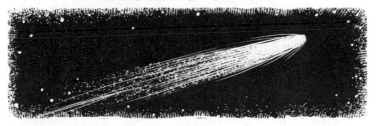

A COMET IS A BRIGHT OBJECT LIKE A STAR IN THE SKY, OFTEN WITH A LONG TAIL. IN NEWTON'S TIME, PEOPLE BELIEVED COMETS WERE SIGNS FROM HEAVEN THAT SOMETHING TERRIBLE (OR WONDERFUL) WAS GOING TO HAPPEN. IN 1682, A BRIGHT COMET APPEARED. NEWTON'S FRIEND EDMOND HALLEY READ OLD REPORTS FROM ASTRONOMERS GOING BACK FOR MANY YEARS. HE NOTICED THAT THERE WERE REPORTS OF SOME KIND OF BRIGHT OBJECT APPEARING IN THE SKY JUST ABOUT EVERY SEVENTY-SIX YEARS. HE MADE A BRILLIANT LEAP AND GUESSED THAT IT WAS ACTUALLY THE SAME COMET COMING BACK OVER AND OVER. THIS WOULD MEAN COMETS ORBITED THE SUN, JUST LIKE THE PLANETS—ONLY COMETS HAD A MUCH LONGER ORBIT. HE PREDICTED THAT IT WOULD APPEAR AGAIN IN 1758. HALLEY WAS ALREADY DEAD BY THEN, BUT WHEN THE COMET REAPPEARED JUST AS HE SAID IT WOULD, IT WAS NAMED IN HIS HONOR.

Chapter 9
Newton's Big Book

Halley's question rekindled Newton's interest in the way planets moved. He wrote a nine-page essay to answer it and then kept on going. "Now that I am upon this subject," he wrote, "I would gladly know the bottom of it." In only eighteen months, he finished his five-hundred-page masterpiece. The title is *Mathematical Principles of Natural Philosophy,* familiarly known from its Latin title as *Principia.* With this book, he laid the foundation of modern physics. Every physicist since 1687 has built their work on the ideas in Newton's book.

Halley was excited. He wanted to make sure Newton didn't keep this revolutionary work to himself. He acted as Newton's editor and even paid for the book to be printed.

Right away, it looked as if there might be trouble. Newton's old enemy, Hooke, claimed that Newton had taken ideas from him. Newton was so furious that he threatened not to publish at all. It took all Halley's tact to calm him down.

The book came out in 1687 and caused a sensation. Readers felt as if the universe had suddenly been explained to them. A French mathematician wondered, "Does Mr. Newton eat, drink, and sleep like other men?" (As we know, the answer to this was actually *no*.)

Probably the book was admired and discussed more than it was actually read. It was almost impossible to follow. Newton even hinted that he had done this deliberately. It was a way to protect himself from people asking stupid questions.

Newton's book made him so famous that he was elected to Parliament. He became a member of the government just in time to vote in favor of the Glorious Revolution of 1689. Except for this one important vote, which brought a new king to the throne of England, he did not take any active role in Parliament. The only time he actually spoke was to ask for a window to be closed.

Chapter 10
Laws of Motion

Over three hundred years after Newton's book was written, it is hard to understand how great its impact has been. The things he figured out now seem natural and obvious to us. This is because Newton completely changed the way people think. Today, even people who have never heard of Newton think of movement in the terms he invented.

What exactly was in his revolutionary book? The idea of gravity, to start with. Earlier, Newton had studied two forces. The first was the one that pulled the apple and the moon toward the Earth. The second was the one that made planets orbit the sun. He realized that these were both the same force. He gave it the name we still use today:

"It is now established that this force is gravity, and therefore we shall call it gravity from now on."

Newton also created his three laws of motion. He had learned the first law from Galileo. It says that if something is moving, it will keep moving until something makes it stop. If something is sitting still, it won't move until some force makes it move.

The second law shows how much force is needed to make something move or stop moving.

The final law says that, "For every action there is an equal and opposite reaction." This means that every time you push on something, it pushes back just as strongly, but in the opposite direction.

If you're standing on a skateboard and you push against the ground, the ground pushes back against you, which is why the skateboard moves forward. Or think of a balloon filled with air. If you let go of the neck of the balloon, the air rushes out of the balloon backward.

This pushes the balloon forward with the same force, so the balloon flies through the air. This same principle makes a rocket's engine work.

Newton's three laws explain the movement of everything in the universe. When combined with a lot of mathematics, these laws can predict everything from tides on Earth to the movement of stars in distant galaxies.

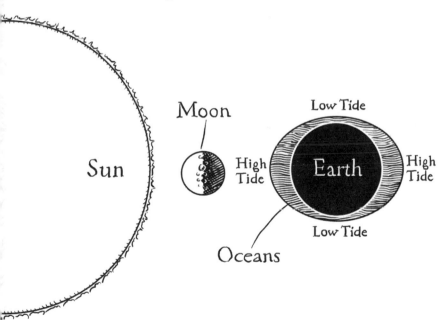

THE MOON AND THE OCEAN'S TIDES

One odd thing is missing from Newton's explanation of gravity. Although he described how gravity acts, he never said exactly what it is. We can't blame him for this—three hundred years later, we still don't really know.

Chapter 11
Becoming a Legend

After his book came out, Newton became legendary. Suddenly Cambridge students saw him in a whole new way. "We gaz'd on him . . . as on someone divine," one recalled.

His life, however, continued more or less unchanged for the next few years. Then in 1693, Newton had a mental breakdown. He couldn't eat or sleep. He wrote his friends strange letters saying he wished they were dead. He accused them of trying to get him in trouble with women.

When he recovered, he decided he needed a change. In 1696, he asked some powerful friends to help him find a new job. They arranged for him to help run the Royal Mint.

THE TOWER OF LONDON

The Mint was the place that created all
England's coins. It was in the Tower of London.
Newton moved into a grand house in London.
His friends expected he would hire someone else
to do most of the work. Instead, Newton threw
himself into the job.

For years, counterfeiters had been clipping bits of silver off the edges of coins to make new coins. By Newton's time, much of England's money was worth less than it was supposed to be. The government had to do something. They decided on the Great Recoinage of 1696.

The Mint collected all the clipped coins and remade them into a new form of coin. These coins had ridged edges, so they were harder to fake. Newton oversaw the whole thing. He did such a good job that in 1699 he was promoted to Master of the

Mint. He stayed in this position for almost thirty years, until he died.

Once the Great Recoinage was done, Newton turned his attention to catching counterfeiters. He made himself into a kind of detective with a network of spies and informers. His greatest triumph was the capture of the clever counterfeiter named Chaloner. Newton pursued him for years and finally succeeded in having him executed.

During his first few years in London, Newton kept his distance from the Royal Society. He didn't want any more fights. In 1703, his old enemy Hooke died. The president of the society died the same year. Newton was immediately elected in his place. In 1704, Newton finally published his theory of optics. The book was based on research from many years earlier, but as he explained, "To avoid being engaged in Disputes about these matters, I have hitherto delayed the printing." He meant that he had waited until Hooke was dead.

Chapter 12
Battles at the Royal Society

Newton ruled the Royal Society like a tyrant. This led to some ugly incidents. The worst was the fight about who really invented calculus. Newton had created his form of calculus, the method of fluxions, as early as 1665, but he had refused to publish it. Only a few carefully chosen people got the chance to see it.

Around 1675, a German mathematician named Gottfried Leibniz had come up with a similar system, which he called calculus. It isn't surprising that someone

GOTTFRIED LEIBNIZ

else would make the same discovery as Newton had. After all, Leibniz had been working on the same kinds of problems. He had even written to Newton about his new kind of mathematics. (Ironically, he began one letter, "How great I think the debt owed you . . .") Leibniz published his paper on calculus in 1684.

At first, there didn't seem to be a problem. Then in 1704, Newton finally published his version of calculus. An anonymous reviewer hinted that he might have borrowed some of Leibniz's ideas.

Newton was furious. He didn't want anyone else to get the credit for inventing calculus. An ugly battle began, with Newton accusing Leibniz of stealing ideas from him. At first Leibniz was reasonable. "Mr. Newton developed it further, but I arrived at it by another way," he wrote to a friend. "One man makes one contribution, another man another."

Newton didn't think this made any difference. "Second inventors," he claimed, "have no right."

Finally in 1711, Leibniz appealed to the Royal Society to settle the fight, but Newton was president of the society. He put himself in charge of the committee looking into the issue. What's more, he secretly wrote the committee's report himself.

Published in 1713, the report twisted the evidence to make it seem that Leibniz had stolen Newton's work. Leibniz died three years later. Newton never regretted what he had done. Years later, he recalled happily that he "had broke Leibniz's Heart."

In one sense, however, Leibniz won the calculus wars. Newton's method of fluxions was a kind of personal shorthand. He never meant it to be used by anyone else. Leibniz's system was easier for other people to understand. Everyone who learns calculus today uses Leibniz's terms, symbols, and methods, not Newton's. Even the name *calculus* is from Leibniz. If Newton knew, he would be furious.

Chapter 13
Genius

Despite being so frail as a baby, Newton lived to be an old man. By his last years he was wealthy, powerful, and respected. In 1705, he was knighted by Queen Anne. He became Sir Isaac Newton.

Newton's mind remained sharp and his health
mostly good almost to the end. He led a meeting
of the Royal Society less than a month before his
death.

He died on March 20, 1727, at age eighty-five. He was buried in London's Westminster Abbey—the first scientist to receive such an honor. The inscription on his fancy marble monument shows what awe he inspired. "Here is buried Isaac Newton, Knight, who by a strength of mind almost divine . . . explored . . . what no other scholar has previously imagined." The great poet Alexander Pope wrote of him: "Nature and Nature's Laws lay hid in Night. God said, 'Let Newton be!' and all was light."

A mind almost divine—this is a grand claim. Still, scientists from Newton's time through our own agree. What Newton accomplished was greater than his individual discoveries. He wanted to understand how everything fit together. It was as if other scholars had written interesting sentences, but Newton figured out the way all these sentences could be put together to tell the story of how the universe worked.

WESTMINSTER ABBEY

BUILDING STARTED ON WESTMINSTER ABBEY IN THE YEAR 1245. KINGS, QUEENS, AND THEIR FAMILIES ARE USUALLY MARRIED AND CROWNED THERE. UNTIL THE 1760S, IT WAS ALSO WHERE MOST OF THEM WERE BURIED. PEOPLE WHO WORKED FOR THE CHURCH WERE ALSO BURIED THERE. STARTING AROUND THE TIME NEWTON WAS A CHILD, BEING BURIED IN WESTMINSTER ABBEY BECAME A WAY TO HONOR SOMEONE FOR SPECIAL ACHIEVEMENTS. GREAT GENERALS, POLITICIANS, POETS, AND MUSICIANS WERE RECOGNIZED IN THIS WAY. ISAAC NEWTON WAS THE FIRST SCIENTIST.

Newton knew that he had only begun to tell this story. As an old man he said, "I don't know what I may seem to the world, but as to myself, I seem to have been only like a boy playing on the sea-shore and diverting myself in now and then finding a smoother pebble or a prettier shell than ordinary, whilst the great ocean of truth lay all undiscovered before me."

For the next two hundred years, almost all physics had its roots in his ideas. Only at the beginning of the twentieth century did another great genius—Albert Einstein—discover the limits of Newton's discoveries. In day-to-day life, however, people rarely have to deal with situations where Newton's physics doesn't make sense. It's still the way we understand the world.

ALBERT EINSTEIN

Whether we are riding a bicycle, catching a baseball, or dropping an apple, most of us most think of movement in terms we learned from that strange, bad-tempered, brilliant loner Isaac Newton.

TIMELINE OF ISAAC NEWTON'S LIFE

1642 —— Isaac Newton is born on December 25

1654 —— Moves to a nearby town to attend grammar school

1661 —— Enters Trinity College, Cambridge

1665 —— Graduates from Cambridge with a BA
Moves back to his mother's farm to escape the plague

1668 —— Receives his master's degree from Cambridge

1669 —— Becomes Lucasian Professor of Mathematics

1671 —— Sends his reflecting telescope to the Royal Society

1672 —— Elected to the Royal Society

1679 —— Newton's mother, Hannah, dies

1684 —— Halley, Hooke, and Wren meet at a coffeehouse to discuss planetary motion

1687 —— Newton's *Principia* published

1689 —— Elected to Parliament

1693 —— Suffers a nervous breakdown.

1696 —— Moves to London to work at the Mint

1699 —— Appointed Master of the Mint

1703 —— Elected President of the Royal Society

1704 —— Publishes his research on optics

1705 —— Knighted

1712 —— The Royal Society establishes a committee to decide who invented calculus

1727 —— Isaac Newton dies, March 20

TIMELINE OF THE WORLD

Civil war breaks out in England — **1642**

The Thirty Years' War ends in Europe — **1648**

King Charles I beheaded, January 30 — **1649**

Charles II restored as king of England — **1660**
Royal Society founded

Robert Hooke invents the word "cell" to describe — **1663**
what he sees in the microscope

Plague breaks out in England — **1665**

Great Fire of London — **1666**

Milton publishes *Paradise Lost* — **1667**

Charleston (originally called Charles Towne) — **1670**
is founded in North America by the British

Pocket watch invented — **1675**

Halley's comet appears — **1682**

Glorious Revolution in England — **1688–1689**

A bill of rights guarantees Englishmen — **1689**
some freedom of speech and religion

The Salem witch trials take place in Massachusetts — **1692**

The Bank of England is established — **1694**

Benjamin Franklin is born — **1706**

The "Great Frost" is the coldest winter in Europe — **1709**
in over five hundred years

First practical steam engine built — **1712**

Janet Horne becomes the last person in Britain — **1727**
to be executed as a witch

BIBLIOGRAPHY

Ackroyd, Peter. **Newton**. New York: Doubleday, 2006.

* Christianson, Gale E. **Isaac Newton and the Scientific Revolution**. New York: Oxford University Press, 1996.

Gleick, James. **Isaac Newton**. New York: Pantheon Books, 2003.

* Krull, Kathleen. **Giants of Science: Isaac Newton**. New York: Viking, 2006.

Westfall, Richard S. **The Life of Isaac Newton**. New York: Cambridge University Press, 1993.

* Books for young readers